LITTLE

HEARTS THAT

BEAT AS ONE

Dora Scott

LITTLE HEARTS THAT BEAT AS ONE

LITTLE HEARTS THAT BEAT AS ONE

Dora Scott

Legacy Publishing
Imagination at Work

ISBN: 978-1-944632-02-1

ISBN: 978-1-944632-01-4

Library of Congress Control Number: 2020932112

ACKNOWLEDGEMENTS

I give honor to my Lord and Savior Jesus Christ above all, who is first in my life. Without him, none of this would be possible. Thank you, Jesus!

My inspiration comes from Maya Angelou, she was the epitome of a famous author and a great writer. I love the fact that Oprah Winfrey and Michelle Obama are brilliant and successful. I am striving to be ambitious and successful. Each and every day, I am getting closer to my goals. My destiny is promised and my future is bright.

I would like to acknowledge one of my dearest friend and sister, Gail Palmorn. All of my motivation comes from her. When no one believed in me when I didn't believe in myself, and I had no one else, GOD used you to speak in and over my life. I love you and appreciate you so much.

DEDICATION

I dedicate this book to my Mom, Marthenia Sarann McGill Marion for giving me a rich experience as a child and for teaching me how to love and share.

I dedicate this book to my children: Lakeisha, Sammy, and my grandchildren: Glenisha, Glen Jr., and GeniYa whom emulate those hearts.

I also dedicate this book to all mothers, especially the Atlanta Housewives.

TABLE OF CONTENTS

Introduction

How important is it to speak over your unborn child? To pray, read, sing, and talk are all essential tools! Preparing your fetus as it goes through the stages of growth inside your womb is priority as well.

Always get proper rest and take your vitamins. Some expecting mothers may attend childbirth classes. Every mother may not be able to afford these classes; however, they may be insured and can also practice some self-care exercise at home.

Most first-time moms don't know what to expect unless they do the research. Another useful option is to speak to an experienced mother, but to speak over your unborn child for the first time will be an incredible experience that you will never forget.

In essence, this book is a declaration of how mothers diligently invest their hearts into the development of their children from infancy to adolescents; a mother's intuition is always on point. I pray this book will bless, enlighten, excite, inspire, intrigue, and uplift everyone and every mother who reads this book.

This book *Little Hearts that Beat as One*, was created in a vision. Even though I have my own personal experience because I birth two children, but my inspiration comes from a vision that GOD gave me.

I was dreaming one day and I woke up hearing a voice saying "little hearts that beat as one" and I ask the Lord,

"What are you saying? What is the meaning of that?"

So the Lord began to speak to me and said, "As I speak, write the vision and make it plain upon tables that he may run that readeth it. Now some of the pages of this book will be very familiar, because every mother, or soon-to-be mothers have had similar experiences, but what makes this book unique is the heart of unity."

Remember what God told man, "Therefore shall a man leave his father and mother, and cleave unto his wife and they shall be one flesh."

So, if man can become one with woman, than most certainly little hearts can beat as one.

Because that's what the world needs: oneness and unity. Why not start with the new generations who have the potential to have such an impact on the world. *Little Hearts that Beat as One* inspires me with just the topic itself. When you read it for the first time, I want it to speak volume!

You have to start somewhere, so why not begin with these precious little hearts. Whenever you start at the beginning of anything, you have a chance to get to the root of it all, and by getting to the root, you have the opportunity to make ongoing changes.

Our children are our future, so if you want a better future, let's start with the ones who will make a difference. With life in general, you want to reach them while they are young and impressionable.

When you can train a child at a young age, you have the opportunity to steer them in the right direction. When they are at a certain age; you have their undivided attention. You will have such an impact on them. For example, anyone looking to adopt children often want a younger child that they can teach or train. When you get someone of age, whose already been raised by someone else, or self-trained, you tend to have problems.

Little Hearts that Beat as One, is an impression of the growth and learning experience of a child, and how hearts beat as one. This book will take you on a journey to be your unique self, and to teach you about growth, and how to become one with your children.

Along the way, parents will see a journey of how your child develop his or her own personal attitude. But of course with help and guidance from the parents. We, as parents never stop caring, loving, and training them to be responsible.

It's your job as a parent to bring out the best in your children, even when they don't feel their best, or look their best. Parents, your opinion means the world to a child, so it's time to equip yourselves and get the tools you need to speak over their lives.

What you think and what you say will have a tremendous impact on your child. So, get it right the first time. You should see and know your children potentials, and their attributes. You should be the first face they wake up to, and the last face they see at night.

From a child perspective, they hold you accountable, because you birth them, you gave them life. So your words mean the world to them. If no one on the outside believes in them, they know they can come home to receive encouragement, and motivation.

Make sure, you as a parent listen to your children. Spend quality time with them, get to know what drives them, what motivates them, be active in their life. Be visible in their life, and show interest in their life. Be number one in their lives. Whatever a child did not receive at home, they have the tendency to find it outside of their homes. It is your responsibility to protect and secure them in every way.

A MOTHER'S INTUITION

A mother's intuition is always on point and she always has her children best interest at heart. Teach your children how to value themselves and how to know their worth. Teach them morals. The key to it all is how to love one another, *Little Hearts that Beat as One*.

Chapter 1

Childbirth - Three Months

The Experience of Motherhood

You have been waiting for this moment for nine months, anticipating this day, it's finally here. Birthing a baby is nothing short of a miracle. You are packed and ready to go. You find moments where you want to speed up the process, but you decide to be patient, even though you are ready to hear her little heartbeat for the first time.

Patience is a virtue. First-time moms tend to be more anxious, either way bringing a life into the world is priceless. Who should be in the delivery room? Of course, if you are married, husband and mom, and close friends who you desire to be there.

You know in these days and times, choosing a baby's name can be exhausting. Most first-time fathers, if the baby is a boy, he will be a Jr. Girls' names have become complicated. You know we don't do the easy and simple names anymore, we have gotten to the point where we name our girls after cars, like Mercedes, Kia, and Lexus.

Anyway you will be anxious to keep reading, because the title of my book is *Little Hearts that Beat as One*, with that being said chapter by chapter, it will come in full fruition.

The stages of labor are different for all mothers. During my time back in the 70's they didn't offer epidurals, so it was natural birth hours of labor pain, or a C-section. Now in this day and time, we have access to epidurals and other options such as home birth, Lamaze birth, and water birth.

Childbirth is one of the most precious moment in the world you want to remember. As a woman you may realize, the nine months during your pregnancy when you were nauseous, vomiting, feeling fatigue, and the list lingers on, it was all worth it.

When your baby finally opens her eyes for the first time, that will be a breath-taking moment, then you gaze into her beautiful eyes, and you begin to reminisce, on what a miracle it is bringing a life into the world.

Now the healing process begins, during your doctor's visits you probably had the conversation with your doctor about breast feeding. I've heard when you breastfeed, you and your baby develop a connection and a bond that's inseparable; the journey begins.

The first three months are very fragile; you can't forget those doctor's appointments. If It's anything like reality television or the celebrities I have watched on television, it's nothing short of a miracle. A miracle comes from above, every good and perfect gift comes from above.

Every day you take time to care and nurture, your newborn, pampering them and you are reluctant to veer away from them. When the baby was in your womb, you constantly massage your belly, speaking blessings over your baby's life. Now that you can gaze into their bright eyes, you just want to capture every moment.

Also, you will serenade soft melodies to them, and when you are feeding them, you are looking into their eyes wondering how you are so blessed. Every waking moment when they cry, you don't want to miss a beat. It's either time to feed, nurture, or change their diaper; or it's just mommy and me time.

You don't want to miss a moment because every stage is vital. The newborn stage is when the baby sleeps all day and keeps you up all night. First-time moms are captivated at every moment and as a mom every waking moment is priceless.

Chapter 2

Three - Six Months

At any age, babies are precious, but fragile until three months and older. Parents get to see the growth process, everything about your baby becomes visual. Proud mom and dad, and if you are grandma or grandpa for the first time, they will captivate your heart.

I had my first experience 21 years ago, and it was priceless. I have three grandchildren now - two girls and a boy, I often tell my grandchildren, whatever mom and dad cannot do or do not want to do, that's where grandparents come in. We try to get them everything their little heart's desire.

The love that mother and father have is incredible, but the love that grandparents have is impeccable. The growth and stages of children is nothing short of a miracle, some children grow faster than others, sometimes babies move fast, because they are getting out the way for another child.

Seventy-five percent of the time this is true, Moms realize they are pregnant again, little hearts coming together. As babies are growing, they begin to move and try to roll over. The fragile stage is nearing an end; a precious child never ceases to amaze you. They begin to form their own image of who they look like. Mom? Dad? Grandma or grandpa?

Of course, mom will say the child looks just like her. Now, the time the infant wakes you up during the night has shorten. You and your baby are getting to know each other. He knows there is a bond, a connection, his eyes follow the very image that he sees.

Precious moments! Your eyes are fixated on them and their eyes on you, another Kodak moment. The idea of capturing every moment is precious of course. At that stage of their precious life, you are taking pictures and recording every memorable moment.

Nurturing the infant at any stage is very important. At the age of six months, your baby is ready for solid food. Your baby is ready to play, listen to sounds, and explore their surroundings. This is the stage where your baby is growing and developing quickly.

I hope you are prepared, because this stage of infancy is when you cannot leave them unattended. A mother's love for her children is what we call agape love. A child will experience love, a child will develop love, a child will know when a mother is communicating love. So, make sure he gets your undeniable and undivided attention.

Chapter 3

Seven - Eleven Months

Your baby is now beginning to develop his own identity. The baby's legs are stronger now and he is able to sit up and support his weight. Wait for it! It's fun time with your baby. Your baby is smiling and laughing more. When you call your baby's name, his little bright eyes open wide.

They have listened to the sound of your voice, for so long, they have an identity. Their little hands are stronger, they can hold and play with toys. When you sing lullabies to your baby, she lights up. The interaction and connection you develop with your baby is breathtaking.

Just like every child is different, every parent is different, some parents start reading to their children when they are infants - bed time stories is the best. Some babies crawl and walk before others, about the age of six to ten months they are ready to crawl, make their first sound besides the sound you are used to.

Now they are ready to say their first word, "Mama" and "Dada". Imagine your baby taking her first step. How exciting is that? Watching your baby take her first step is the moment you've been waiting for. Celebrities, hard working moms sometimes miss this important moment, because the child is either with the nanny or at a daycare, but that's what those cameras or camcorders are for.

Developing Independence:

Housewives and stay-at-home moms never miss a moment, they are up on everything, capturing every Kodak moment. At this age a baby has already developed his identity, you now know if he will need all of your attention, or you can watch from a distance, meaning if he will interact with other children.

A child needs to interact with other children. Parents please understand "kids will be kids", they will play together for a while, then they will want to push and hit. That is the typical way of a child, but remember the best kind of training is home training, everything begins at home.

Home is where the heart is, and charity begins at home. You know they always say, you can tell if a child has been trained at home, speaking of their behavior outside of the home.

I have a niece named Priscilla and her first child, Zola is attached to her. Zola is two years old. What I want to emphasize is how to free yourself if your baby is overly-attached to you. That can be a good or bad thing. The good part is you don't have to worry about your child being abducted or taken, because you are always with her.

The bad thing is you can't get away from your child for important reasons, or have free time for yourself. Your baby will not have the opportunity to engage or interact with others, which can be problematic in the future when your child should be growing in independence. So, give your child many opportunities to spend time with people you love and trust such as aunts, uncles, grandmas, and grandpas.

My nephew CJ is eleven months, he's a model baby.

When you are destined to become a mom or dad, you have tried everything, and then a miracle happens! My nephew Elder Calvin and his wife have a baby boy named CJ, Calvin Jr. He is so intelligent; his Daddy reads and talks to him. CJ is a model baby; he is very attentive, CJ will smile, laugh, and get all happy like he understands what his dad is talking about.

Are you looking for a miracle? Have you been praying and working towards having your own baby? Don't lose heart! If God did it for my nephew Calvin and his wife, he can do it for you too.

Chapter 4

One – Three-Years-Old

This is the most exciting time in your life preparing for your baby to turn one. The excitement of planning their first birthday party is overwhelming, but you got this. Who's invited? Probably every toddler in the neighborhood, whether you make plans to have it at your house, or rent a building, it will be memorable.

When you are preparing for your baby's first birthday party, the excitement begins. Your baby does not quite understand. She is excited that she is walking, you are excited also, making plans, finding the perfect cake, and the perfect theme. It's your baby's first birthday party, you are ecstatic, because you have been anticipating this moment, you are ready.

When you are planning your baby's first birthday party: the guest list and entertainment are fun, although your baby doesn't understand what's going on. But, that's just what makes it exciting.

When every mom plans the first birthday party, they figure out it's best to order two cakes: one big exquisite cake for the guests, and one little miniature animated cake for the baby.

While entertaining your guests, it's time for the big moment, all cameras, tablets, camcorders, and IPhones are all on the baby. When you set the cake in-front of the baby, we all sing happy birthday. Your baby lights up, then her precious little hands dive into the cake.

First into her mouth, now all over her face and everywhere else... developing independence. This is when the title of this story begins, *Little Hearts that Beat as One*. This is when you train and teach your child how to interact with other children. They don't quite understand how to share, but that's where every parent comes in.

"Train your children in the way they should go, and when they get old, it will not depart from them." As you surround your child with other children, they will learn to socialize, especially in daycare. They will learn how to play and interact with others. Some children are very selfish, but you as a parent have to teach them how to share.

Of course they will cry and throw a fit, but you are the one who they will listen to, teach them and show them. The more you care, the more you will share. Most parents began to potty-train their children at age two; at this stage you must prepare them to become a big boy, or a big girl.

What we call training pants, or pull- ups are the tools parents use to make this process easier. Every time your children uses the potty; you should reward them. Potty-training for boys and girls are different. For me training my girl was easier; some say the boys are easier, but either way, get ready for a real experience.

My niece KT will have to start this potty-training process very soon because her twins are growing quickly. There was a time we were very afraid for the boy because he was premature. They were born at 36 weeks. She named them Sir Kylan and Princess Kayleigh. He weighed four pounds and eight ounces; she weighed five pounds and eleven ounces.

My nephew Kylan struggled with gaining weight, but with breast-feeding, he started putting on more weight. His pediatrician put him on a special formula called Elecare. Then their caring and loving mom, KT went above and beyond to nurse them to good health. Sir Kylan has double his sized. Now, they are growing and are very active -- getting into everything.

My other nephew Allen Jr. has a daughter named Alura Marie Smith, she just turned a year old in January. She started crawling probably between five to six months. I witnessed Alura, crawling up their stairways at six months. It showed the strength of a little angel; she started walking at eight months. My nieces and nephew are definitely a part of the title of my book: *Little Heart That Beat as One*.

Chapter 5

Three - Five-Years-Old

This is the stage where you have to be careful what you say around your toddlers, because they will repeat everything they hear. It is very essential that you speak and say positive thing around them, while you are in your training mode.

It's vital that you teach them at this stage how to interact with other children. When you teach your child how to play and interact with others, it makes it easier when they are in daycare, or in preschool. At the age of four and five jump start their day; get them ready in the morning for preschool. That's one of the most exciting time. Now, you can create memories that will last a lifetime.

We have a five-year-old living in our home, so we know what it's like. Some days she is excited about school; some mornings she's upset because she has to go to school, but that comes with being a five-year-old.

Her name is Aysia and she loves to share and play with others. As a parent or caregiver, you have to remind them how important it is to get along with others, how to give, how to share, how to love, and how to care.

We live in a world where there are negative things going on, so you want to always surround your children in a safe, secure, and a positive environment. This is also the age where they are curious to learn. Parents, you have the willpower, never let go. You are in control.

They are at the age where they can learn; children are much smarter and wiser than before. Let's start teaching them how to get along with others, and how to love others. Set examples for your children, and be a positive role model.

In order for their little hearts to beat as one, they need to see the same attributes in their parents. How can I teach you something I've never experienced? That's what most parents will say as an excuse, but because of the time we are living in, you have a chance to make a difference in your children's life and in others.

We were taught how to become one. We know what creating an environment of people in unison is all about. If for some reason someone missed the mark, it's not because they were not taught. It's simply because they are caught up in a selfish world that needs change.

This new generation has the opportunity to change the world by uniting with one another. I am my brother's keeper, and I am my sister's keeper. Together we make every heart beat as one. It's not the size of the heart; it's not the depths of the heart; it's the love that's in the heart that causes the blood to flow through your veins. Your heart and my heart...they are united and flowing with love...NOW, our little hearts beat as one.

Chapter 6

Six-Years-Old

A six-year-old is ready to be responsible. Make them be responsible for cleaning their rooms, picking up after themselves. This will help them as they get older; these little hearts are ready to expand.

Probably at this age, they are ready for sleepovers, so of course they have to learn how to share, and to play well with others. They are ready to share all their toys, play station etc., this is the way little hearts beat as one!

Being a team player, a team member, or being on a team such as baseball/football, other sports requires the understanding of sharing. For a girl, it will be softball, girl scout, cheerleading. A mentor/coach will teach you, you are never alone. You will learn how to make friends, and how to be friendly.

My niece Marshun is six years young, I think in every family, we have that child that acts funny. Shaunie is the one, but with the help of her Mom,

Shaunie little  ⧠ will become one with others.

Proverbs 18:24 says, "A man that hath friends, must first show himself friendly.   There is a friend that sticks closer than a brother. A six-year old is probably in the first grade, so when you're at school this is the time to show yourself friendly. Once you get to know your classmates, you already know who is going to be your best friend.

This is the time when you ask mom or dad if they can come over for dinner, and during dinner, if they can stay over. Now you know that your little heart beat is one, you have made friends, and you are ready to share.

How do little hearts beat as one?

You must have the same beat! You must listen to the same beat! You must play the same beat! One beat, one sound. First, you are taught by your parents, they train you how to act and how to believe in yourself at a young age. They teach you how to be courteous, how to love yourself and others, how to be friendly, how to make friends, how to take care of yourself, and how to share. My heart beats for yours, your heart beats for mine, our hearts beat together.

We may be different in beliefs, culture, religions, and race; we may all look completely different on the outside, but on the inside our hearts beat love! On the inside, little hearts beat as one. *Little Hearts that Beat as One*, will come into full fruition in chapter 7.

Chapter 7 will go into more details, little hearts is a selective group of children that will not settle for nothing less. They want the best, and the best is when we become one. We are in the world to make the world better. We are the children that will make a difference, by helping one another, by believing in one another, by listening to one another, by giving, and by living.

At age of five to six, you can begin to have bedtime stories with your toddlers. Let's start by telling the story of little hearts that beat as one.

"Once upon a time, there was a little girl, that stayed in the city. Her family was wealthy. She had everything she could possibly want and more."

Her mom always drives her to school, but on that particular day, she wanted to walk to school. On her way to school, she met a little boy who wasn't well-dressed. He was not well-dressed, because his family was poor. But they did their best to provide for the little boy. Right away she knew he was different from her.

Maybe the clothes that he was wearing was not quite appropriate, but that didn't stop the little girl from wanting to find out why they were different. While at school, some kids treated him different; they didn't want to be around him, but the little girl tried to become his friend."

"He said to her, 'why are you so nice to me, and you don't distance yourself from me like the others.'"

"She said to him, 'even though we might be different and we may dress differently, I was given a silver spoon from birth, and your parents had to struggle. Many will judge you from the outside, but we are the same on the inside. You have a heart and I have a heart. Your heart beats the same as mine.'"

She said to him one day, "Every boy and girl will understand you didn't choose your family, your family chose you. One day we will learn not to look down on an individual, because of the way they look on the outside, but we embrace one another just the way we are'"

And she did, even at school she always let others know, he is my friend. I never looked at him from his outer appearance, because I realize we are the same on the inside. Now everyone see we are together, and they want to know why? I can tell them why his heart beats; my heart beats. Now our hearts beat as one.

Chapter 7:

Seven-Years-Old

How can you be perfect in an imperfect world? We can start with making the world a better place, by creating an environment of unity. A seven-year-old does not know too much about unity, but he understands what a symbol of a heart means. Most people understand that a heart is symbolical for love, so they know that a heart simply means love.

Little Hearts that Beat as One indicates love. What brings the hearts together is love. The cover of the book perfectly illustrates this concept of unity. Seven hearts, each heart is connected, and the heart starts off small, and each heart gets bigger than the next. Can you imagine seven hearts connecting together? The connection is love, and love is what makes the heart grow stronger.

Now that we know about the little hearts that beat as one, let's get into the life of a seven-year-old.

The number seven is symbolical for completeness and divine perfection. Every generation is different, so it's up to the parents to train and nurture their children. The environment they dwell and participate in can sometimes determine their future.

So, you have to make it your business to know who their friends are? Where they hang out? What television programs they watch or what games they play. Be Careful what you say around your children, even when they are younger, because they will emulate your very words.

Parents, it's vital to be a positive role model, discipline begins at home; home is where the heart is. How does a heartbeat as one? or become one? UNITY! Where there is unity, there is strength! Strength that becomes so powerful that it breaks every barrier. Together seven hearts will beat as one.

We should have the same mindset, to prepare our children for the world, because they may not be ready for the world, but the world is always ready and willing to take your children innocence in so many ways.

Please don't let your children become a statistic! You love your children and cherish them, make sure they have everything they need, so they will not go looking and lurking outside their homes.

Great minds think alike, so now they are ready for their own cell phone, play station, etc. We have technology that improves on a day-by-day basis, even your young children are introduce to cell phones, social media, and play station etc.

You should always monitor your children no matter what age they are, because we are living in an unpredictable world, and we have to be careful what we allow into our children ears and spirit. Children are always anxious and ready to get into something.

The best thing you can do for your children is to have a lock on everything. You may think at a young age, it's not necessary to monitor your children, but if you don't, there is a possibility they will be exposed to things that will take your breath away.

At their young precious and innocent age, anything a child can possibly imagine, you can google it. The internet and networks know no age. If they are experienced or smart enough to use a cell phone, a laptop, or a notebook, then they have access to the world systems.

At the age of accountability is when you start training your child, proverbs 22:6, "train up your child in the way they should go, and when they get old, it will not depart from them. This is probably the age where they are asking for allowance. Make sure you have chores for your children, where they can earn their allowances.

Always reward them when they do good deeds, when they do their homework, or when they make good grades in school. Let them know how proud you are, how much you appreciate every effort, and how much you love them every day.

You may be wondering why I chose seven chapters? The number seven is completion. A seven-year-old does not know anything about love, other than what mom and dad have shown and taught them every day. It is essential and vital that you tell your children how much you love them every single day.

You tell them, "I love you."

Then they say in return, "I love you, mom! I love you, dad!"

Now that you have experience how to be a seven-year-old, and what's expected of you, I now, know love, I know my heart beats love.

My heart beat is the number seven. It's bigger and better, stronger and full of LOVE. My number is seven. When we all come together, we will make a difference. Every creed, every culture, every language, every race- will come together to make a difference. There is room in this space, for every heart that's connected and has made a tremendous impact on growth. When you give your heart and share, it shows how much you care, *Little Hearts that Beat as One*! Now my book is finally done, I am happy to say *Little Hearts Beat as One*!

THE END!

ABOUT THE AUTHOR

A native Floridian, Dora Ann Scott, is an author and an influential leader in her ministry. Her compassion to help others achieve their spiritual development is what catapulted her to start writing her book.

She is married to Philip Scott for the past 25 years and has two beautiful children, Lakisha Lewter (teacher) and Sammy McGriff (musician). She is an innovative and visionary leader who directed Sisters with a Mission for 12 years. She is a dedicated member and deaconess at the Bible of Church of God for the past 35 years.

She serves under the leadership of Bishop Bobby Banks and First Lady Gloria Banks. Dora loves working with young ladies and seeing them reach their highest potential. Her mission is to utilize her book to encourage and motivate parents to see the value of nurturing unity within relationships.

Simplicity, generosity, and integrity of spirit are few in many, but this exceptional woman walks in excellence in every area of her life and compels other to do likewise.

You can connect with her at

https://www.facebook.com/dora.scott.71

Other Books by Legacy Publishing

Becoming a Conqueror: How to Keep the Past from Invading Your Present and Destroying Your Future

Get your copy for free at www.drgege.com